The World's Greatest
Paper Airplanes

Designed by Bill Foster of Albarella & Associates, Inc.
Edited by Kristin Ellerbusch.

Distributed to schools and libraries
in the United States by
ENCYCLOPAEDIA BRITANNICA EDUCATIONAL CORP.
310 South Michigan Ave.
Chicago, Illinois 60604

Library of Congress Cataloging-in-Publication Data

Murray, Peter, 1952 Sept. 29-
The world's greatest paper airplanes/
by Peter Murray.
p. cm.
Summary: Instructions for making several kinds
of paper airplanes.
ISBN 0-89565-963-8
1. Paper airplanes — Juvenile literature.
[1. Paper airplanes.]
I. Title.
TL778.M87   1992
645.592 — dc20   92-6004
                                              CIP
                                              AC

The World's Greatest
Paper Airplanes

Written by Peter Murray

Illustrated by Anastasia Mitchell

UMBRELLA BOOKS

THE CHILD'S WORLD

The Original Paper Airplane

Paper was invented in China thousands of years ago. Sometime later, the first paper airplane was launched. The original paper airplane may have looked something like this.

The original paper airplane did not go very far, but it was easy to make. Millions of them still land in wastebaskets every day.

What's that? You say a crumpled up piece of paper is not a "paper airplane?" Even though it is made of paper and it flies through the air?

If that's what you think, you're right. You can throw a rock, but that doesn't mean a rock is an airplane.

A true paper airplane

will *glide* through the air. It has a front end and a back end. It has wings that cut through the air and give it *lift*. Lift is what keeps the airplane up in the air. The original paper airplane did not have much lift.

Some paper airplanes will travel fifty feet with only a gentle throw.

Some will make loop–the–loops.

And some don't fly very well at all, but they look cool.

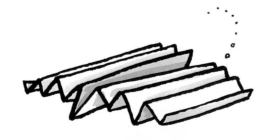

This model flew only three feet before crashing on the floor. But it looked great on the way down.

Paper airplanes come in many different sizes and shapes. In 1967 a magazine called *The Scientific American* had a contest to see who could build the best paper airplanes. They called it the Great International Paper Airplane Contest. Over 11,000 paper airplanes were entered. Some of them did not look like airplanes at all.

But all of them had one thing in common. They all had some kind of a wing. In fact, one of the winners was just a plain wing with no tail and no nose.

Wings come in many shapes, but they all have one thing in common.

The front of the wing, the part that cuts through the air, is always heavier and thicker than the back of the wing. This gives the airplane *lift*.

Your Basic Flying Wing

Constructing The Wing

To make *The Wing*, start with an 8 1/2 x 11 inch sheet of paper.

1 Make a fold about two inches from one end.

2 Then fold the folded part in half.

3 Then fold the folded part over.

4 Now fold the whole thing in half the other way to make a crease down the middle

5 Now shape the wing. Roll it up into a short tube.

6 Flatten it out, then your wing should have a gentle curve.

When it has a nice rounded shape, it is ready to fly.
You might have to do some adjusting to get the curve
just right. It can drive you crazy, but it's worth it.

Flying The Wing

To fly *The Wing*, hold it by the back edge and give it a gentle push through the air. Don't try to throw it hard—it will only crash to the ground.

A carefully sailed wing can stay in the air for a long time. One version of a flying wing flew for over ten seconds and won the International Paper Airplane Contest for "Duration Aloft."

IT'S SO BEAUTIFUL!

Variations

It's easy to make different kinds of wings. You can make a bat-wing.

Or a bird-wing.

Or you can make your wing fly straighter by bending up the tips to form *stabilizers*.

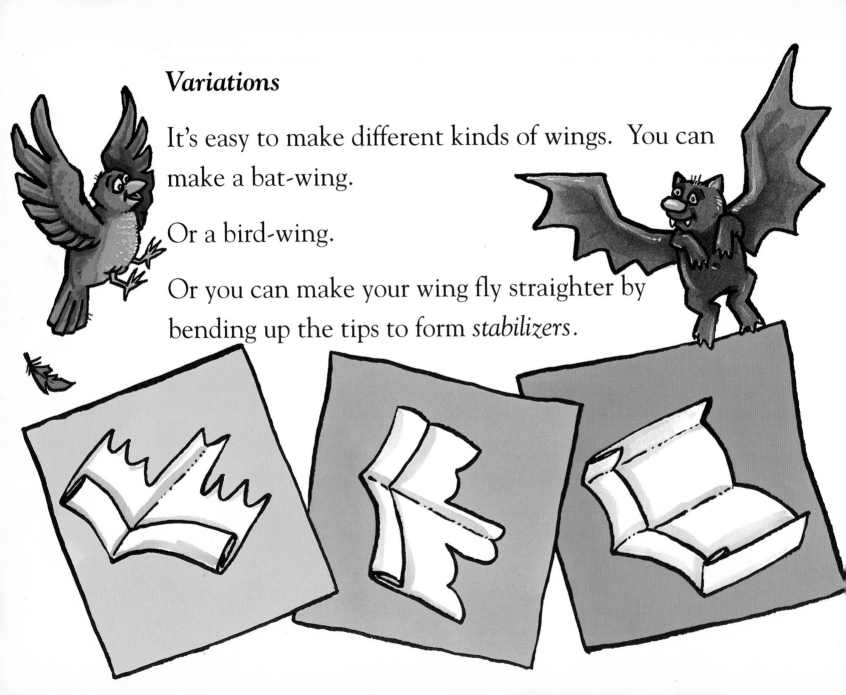

Stabilizers keep your airplane from sliding sideways in the air. They are like wings, but they go up and down instead of sideways. Try flying your plane without stabilizers, then bend up the tips of the wings and try it with stabilizers. Bending the stabilizers different ways will change the way the airplane flies.

Going for Distance

If you want a paper airplane that will fly over a house, build a delta–wing model. There are lots of ways to make them, but they all come out looking something like this.

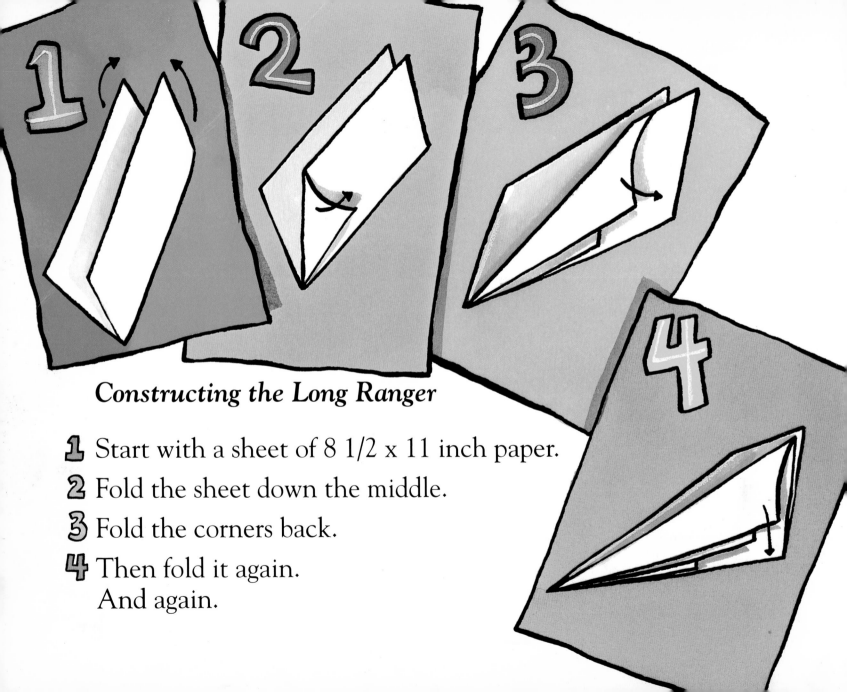

Constructing the Long Ranger

1 Start with a sheet of 8 1/2 x 11 inch paper.
2 Fold the sheet down the middle.
3 Fold the corners back.
4 Then fold it again.
  And again.

Put a little piece of tape across the wings for extra speed and distance.

Cut off the very tip so you won't poke somebody in the eye.
Put a paper clip or two on the front end to balance the airplane.

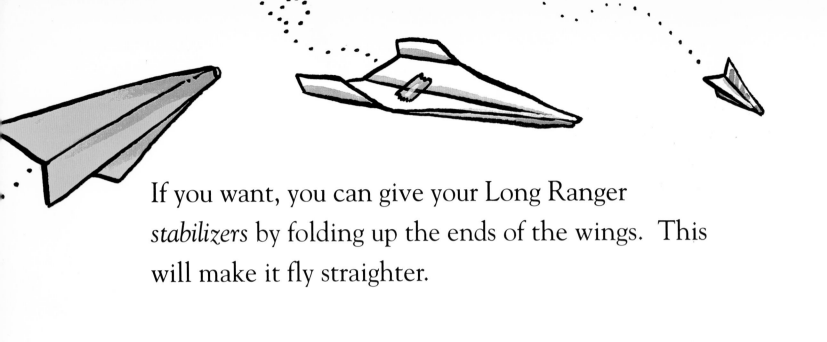

If you want, you can give your Long Ranger *stabilizers* by folding up the ends of the wings. This will make it fly straighter.

Decoration is optional. If you give your airplane a special design, it might even fly better.

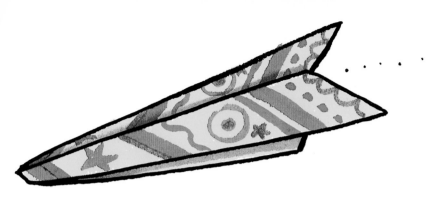

Flying the Long Ranger

A Delta–wing airplane should be thrown hard.
Take it outside. Throw it hard and high!

Constructing the Trickster

For a really wild ride, build yourself a *Trickster*. This basic design can be made in all kinds of different shapes. The basic *Trickster* goes something like this.

Start by making a thin fold at one end of a sheet of paper.

Fold it again.

And again.

And again.

And again.

And again.

You could keep on folding, or you could stop here. The idea is to use up about half the paper this way. When you've decided to stop making these little folds, fold the whole sheet of paper in half the other way.

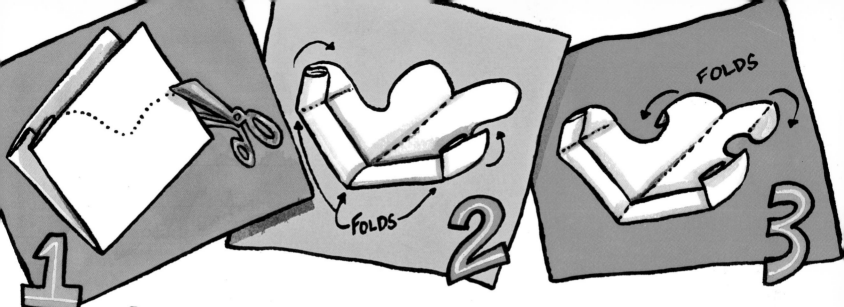

1 Now you can cut out the wing and tail shapes. Shaping them different ways will change the way the airplane flies.

2 Open the paper and give your airplane *stabilizers* by folding up the ends of the wings.

3 Do the same for the tail, but fold the stabilizers down instead of up.

Or you could do it the opposite way. The *Trickster* is not picky.

Flying the Trickster

Hold the Trickster by the tail and give it a gentle push. The *Trickster* will do strange things. You can change the way it flies by changing the shape of the wings or the way the stabilizers are bent. If your *Trickster* keeps diving straight down, you might need to add *elevators* to the tail section. When the elevators are bent up, the air will push the tail section down and the airplane will fly level. Try it and see.

THESE ARE ELEVATORS!

With a little practice you can make the Trickster do whatever you want. Experiment. Try to make it come back to you. Don't forget to decorate it.

Building and flying paper airplanes looks easy, but it takes practice.

Little changes in the shape of the wings can make a big difference in how the airplane flies. The weight of the paper makes a difference too. Even the way you throw it can make a big difference. Some models will go farther with a gentle push, while others need to be thrown as hard as possible.

Remember, if your paper airplane does not turn out the way you dreamed it would, it's easy to start over. If your airplane won't fly no matter what you do, you can always turn it into the original paper airplane.

And start over again.